Best-Loved
AMISH COOKING

Publications International, Ltd.

Front cover photography by Waterbury Creative.

Pictured on the front cover *(clockwise from upper right):* Corn Bread *(page 62),* Country Buttermilk Biscuits *(page 64),* Farmer-Style Sour Cream Bread *(page 68),* Smucker's® Three Bean Salad with Sweet and Sour Apricot Dressing *(page 59),* Fresh Berry Cobbler Cake *(page 76)* and Roasted Chicken with Maple Glaze *(page 20).*
Pictured on the back cover *(clockwise from upper left):* Iowa Corn Pudding *(page 48),* Old-Fashioned Beef Stew *(page 36)* and Country Chicken Pot Pie *(page 26).*

ISBN: 0-7853-3565-X

Manufactured in U.S.A.

8 7 6 5 4 3 2 1

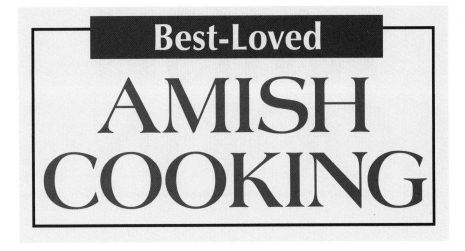

AMISH COOKING

The Amish, a religious group that traces its roots to 16th century Europe, have caught the attention of many Americans because of their chosen lifestyle. They live a simple life, free from much of the stress of contemporary Americans. They shun many of the material goods of modern society, choosing horse-drawn buggies over automobiles, the glow of lamp light over electricity, plain clothes over contemporary styles, and visiting in person rather than over the telephone. Many Amish prefer to farm in Amish communities, usually avoiding much of modern farm technology. Visitors to Amish communities come out of curiosity about this quaint society but leave with respect for a fundamental and uncomplicated way of life.

The Amish people came to America over 200 years ago, bringing with them their native German and Swiss foods. Many of the foods they enjoy today, such as sausage, ham, pork, cabbage, sauerkraut and dumplings, show this heritage; the influence of their American roots is also evident in their love of casseroles, chowders, salads, quick breads, pies and cookies. Many recipes have

been handed down from generation to generation. Food is always abundant, plain and delicious. Amish vegetable gardens, orchards and farms provide many recipe ingredients. This doesn't mean to imply that Amish cooks avoid grocery stores. In fact, they need staples, such as

sugar, flour, chocolate, rice, coffee, tea and salt, and like most Americans find convenience foods such as packaged cereals, cheese, condensed soups, pasta, flavored gelatin and luncheon meats important. Because of their commitment to hard physical work, the Amish have a tradition of enjoying hearty foods. However, today many Amish cooks are looking for ways to serve healthier meals and they are modifying their favorite recipes by reducing fat.

Food is an important part of Amish social gatherings. A table laden with mouthwatering fare is a wonderful way to express their hospitality to friends and family. Whether it's a barn raising, family reunion, wedding dinner or Sunday gathering of friends, there is always plenty of unpretentious soul-satisfying food and drink. An Amish cook never sends anyone home hungry.

This collection of *Best-Loved Amish Cooking* will give you a glimpse of the traditional homey cooking of these plain people. You'll find hearty main dishes, soups and casseroles, well-loved vegetable side dishes and breads, luscious cakes, cobblers and crisps, and tasty pies and cookies. With this cookbook you too can enjoy the heartfelt Amish tradition of food—simple and delicious food that is good for the soul as well as the body.

MEAT & POULTRY

GLAZED ROAST PORK LOIN WITH CRANBERRY STUFFING

- 1¼ cups chopped fresh or partially thawed frozen cranberries
- 2 teaspoons sugar
- ½ cup butter or margarine
- 1 cup chopped onion
- 1 package (8 ounces) herb-seasoned stuffing mix
- 1 cup chicken broth
- ½ cup diced peeled orange
- 1 egg, beaten
- ½ teaspoon grated orange peel
- 1 (2½- to 3-pound) boneless center cut loin pork roast
- ¼ cup currant jelly
- 1 tablespoon cranberry liqueur (optional)

Toss cranberries with sugar. Melt butter in saucepan over medium heat. Add onion; cook and stir until tender. Combine stuffing mix, broth, orange, egg and orange peel in large bowl. Add cranberry mixture and onion; toss.

Preheat oven to 325°F. To butterfly roast, cut lengthwise down roast almost to, but not through bottom. Open like a book. Pound roast with flat side of meat mallet; spread with part of stuffing. Close halves; tie roast with cotton string at 2-inch intervals. Place leftover stuffing in covered casserole; bake during last 45 minutes of roasting time. Place roast on meat rack. Insert meat thermometer.

Combine jelly and liqueur. Brush half of mixture over roast after first 45 minutes. Roast 30 minutes more or until internal temperature reaches 155°F; brush with remaining jelly mixture. Transfer roast to cutting board; tent with foil. Let stand 10 to 15 minutes.

Makes 8 to 10 servings

Glazed Roast Pork Loin with Cranberry Stuffing

BEEF AND PARSNIP STROGANOFF

1 cube beef bouillon
¾ cup boiling water
¾ pound well-trimmed boneless top round beef steak, 1 inch thick
Nonstick olive oil cooking spray
2 cups cubed peeled parsnips or potatoes*
1 medium onion, halved and thinly sliced
¾ pound mushrooms, sliced
2 teaspoons minced garlic
¼ teaspoon black pepper
¼ cup water
1 tablespoon plus 1½ teaspoons all-purpose flour
3 tablespoons reduced-fat sour cream
1½ teaspoons Dijon mustard
¼ teaspoon cornstarch
1 tablespoon chopped fresh parsley
4 ounces cholesterol-free wide noodles, cooked, drained and kept hot

If using potatoes, cut into 1-inch chunks; add to slow cooker with mushroom mixture.

SLOW COOKER DIRECTIONS

1. Dissolve bouillon cube in ¾ cup boiling water; cool. Meanwhile, cut steak into 2×½-inch strips. Spray large nonstick skillet with cooking spray; heat over high heat. Cook and stir beef about 4 minutes or until meat begins to brown and is barely pink. Transfer beef and juices to slow cooker.

2. Spray same skillet with cooking spray; heat over high heat. Add parsnips and onion; cook and stir until browned, about 4 minutes. Add mushrooms, garlic and pepper; cook and stir until mushrooms are tender, about 5 minutes. Add mushroom mixture to slow cooker; mix well.

3. Blend ¼ cup water and flour in small bowl until smooth. Stir flour mixture into cooled bouillon. Add to slow cooker. Cook, covered, on LOW 4½ to 5 hours or until beef and parsnips are tender.

4. Blend sour cream, mustard and cornstarch in medium bowl. Gradually add a little cooking liquid to sour cream mixture; stir well to blend. Stir sour cream mixture into beef mixture. Heat on HIGH until sauce thickens. Sprinkle with parsley; serve over noodles. Garnish, if desired.

Makes 4 servings

Beef and Parsnip Stroganoff

ROAST PORK CHOPS WITH APPLE AND CABBAGE

3 teaspoons olive oil, divided
½ medium onion, thinly sliced
1 teaspoon dried thyme leaves
2 cloves garlic, minced
4 pork chops, 1 inch thick
    (6 to 8 ounces each)
    Salt and pepper
¼ cup cider vinegar
1 tablespoon packed brown
    sugar
¼ teaspoon pepper
1 large McIntosh apple,
    chopped
½ (8-ounce) package
    preshredded coleslaw mix

1. Heat 2 teaspoons oil in large skillet over medium-high heat until hot. Add onion; cook, covered, 4 to 6 minutes or until tender, stirring often. Add thyme and garlic; stir 30 seconds. Transfer to small bowl; set aside.

2. Add 1 teaspoon oil to skillet. Sprinkle pork chops with salt and pepper. Place in skillet; cook 2 minutes per side or until browned. Transfer pork chops to plate. Cover and refrigerate up to 1 day.

3. Remove skillet from heat. Add vinegar, sugar and ¼ teaspoon pepper; stir to dissolve sugar and scrape cooked bits from skillet. Pour mixture into large bowl. Add onion mixture, apple and cabbage; *do not stir.* Cover and refrigerate up to 1 day.

4. To complete recipe, preheat oven to 375°F. Place cabbage mixture in large ovenproof skillet. Heat over medium-high heat; stir until blended and liquid comes to a boil. Lay pork chops on top of cabbage mixture, overlapping to fit. Cover pan; place in oven. Bake 15 minutes or until pork chops are juicy and just barely pink in center.

Makes 4 servings

Make-Ahead Time: up to 1 day in refrigerator
Final Cook Time: 20 minutes

Note: Instead of making ahead, prepare recipe through step 2 as directed above using ovenproof skillet, but do not refrigerate pork chops. Combine vinegar mixture, onion mixture, apple and cabbage in skillet; bring to a boil and top with pork chops. Complete recipe as directed.

Roast Pork Chop with Apple and Cabbage

ZIGEUNERSCHNITZEL

4 tablespoons all-purpose flour, divided
½ teaspoon salt
¼ teaspoon white pepper
4 boneless sirloin pork cutlets (¾ to 1 pound), pounded to ¼-inch thickness
3 tablespoons vegetable oil, divided
1 onion, chopped
1 green bell pepper, diced
1 tomato, peeled, seeded and chopped
1 teaspoon mild or hot paprika
1 cup beef broth
1 to 2 tablespoons whipping cream (optional)

1. Combine 2 tablespoons flour, salt and white pepper in shallow bowl. Coat pork with flour mixture, shaking off excess.

2. Heat 1 tablespoon oil in large skillet over medium-high heat. Cook pork in batches 2 to 3 minutes per side or until golden brown and barely pink in center. Remove from skillet; keep warm.

3. Reduce heat to medium. Add 1 tablespoon oil. Add onion and bell pepper. Cook and stir 10 minutes. Add tomato; cook 5 minutes. Remove vegetables from skillet and set aside.

4. To prepare gravy, heat remaining 1 tablespoon oil in skillet over medium heat until hot. Stir in remaining 2 tablespoons flour and paprika. Cook and stir 1 minute. Whisk in beef broth. Cook and stir about 3 minutes or until thickened; cook 1 to 2 minutes more. Stir in whipping cream, if desired. Add pork and vegetables; heat through.

Makes 4 servings

HERBED ROAST

1 beef top round roast (about 3 pounds)
⅓ cup Dijon-style mustard
1½ teaspoons dried thyme, crushed
1 teaspoon dried rosemary, crushed
1 teaspoon LAWRY'S® Seasoned Pepper
1 teaspoon LAWRY'S® Garlic Powder with Parsley
½ teaspoon LAWRY'S® Seasoned Salt

Brush all sides of roast with mustard. In small bowl, combine remaining ingredients; sprinkle on top and sides of roast, pressing into meat. Place roast, fat side up, on rack in roasting pan. Roast in 325°F oven, 50 minutes to 1 hour or until internal temperature reaches 160°F. Remove roast from oven. Let stand, covered, 15 minutes.   *Makes 6 to 8 servings*

Serving Suggestion: Slice thinly and serve with roasted potato wedges and steamed vegetables.

Zigeunerschnitzel

BAKED HAM WITH SWEET AND SPICY GLAZE

1 (8-pound) bone-in smoked half ham
Sweet and Spicy Glaze (recipe follows)

Preheat oven to 325°F. Place ham, fat side up, on rack in roasting pan. Insert meat thermometer into thickest part of ham away from fat or bone. Roast ham in oven about 3 hours.

Prepare Sweet and Spicy Glaze. Remove ham from oven. Generously brush half of glaze over ham; return to oven 30 minutes longer or until meat thermometer registers 160°F. Remove ham from oven and brush with remaining glaze. Let ham stand about 20 minutes before slicing.   *Makes 8 to 10 servings*

SWEET AND SPICY GLAZE

¾ cup packed brown sugar
⅓ cup cider vinegar
¼ cup golden raisins
1 can (8¾ ounces) sliced peaches in heavy syrup, drained, chopped and syrup reserved
1 tablespoon cornstarch
¼ cup orange juice
1 can (8¼ ounces) crushed pineapple in syrup, undrained
1 tablespoon grated orange peel
1 clove garlic, crushed
½ teaspoon crushed red pepper flakes
½ teaspoon grated fresh ginger

Combine brown sugar, vinegar, raisins and peach syrup in medium saucepan. Bring to a boil over high heat; reduce to low and simmer 8 to 10 minutes. In small bowl, dissolve cornstarch in orange juice; add to brown sugar mixture. Add remaining ingredients; mix well. Cook over medium heat, stirring constantly, until mixture boils and thickens. Remove from heat.
Makes about 2 cups

Baked Ham with Sweet and Spicy Glaze

CHICKEN PAPRIKA

3 tablespoons all-purpose
flour
1 tablespoon paprika
¼ teaspoon salt
⅛ teaspoon black pepper
4 chicken breasts, skinned
(about 1½ pounds)
1 teaspoon olive oil
1 medium onion, chopped
1 cup chicken broth
¼ cup sour cream
Hot cooked spaetzle or
noodles
Fresh parsley (optional)

Combine flour, paprika, salt and
pepper on waxed paper. Coat
chicken breasts with flour mixture.
Reserve remaining flour mixture.

Heat oil in large skillet over
medium heat. Add chicken; cook
about 10 minutes or until
browned on all sides. Remove
chicken from skillet.

Add onion to same skillet; cook
2 minutes. Stir in remaining flour
mixture. Gradually stir in chicken
broth; cook and stir until mixture
comes to a boil. Return chicken to
skillet. Reduce heat to low; cover
and simmer 25 minutes or until
juices run clear.

Remove chicken to platter. Spoon
off fat from gravy in skillet. Add
sour cream to skillet; stir to
combine. Serve with spaetzle.
Garnish with fresh parsley, if
desired.   *Makes 4 servings*

TURKEY WITH CHILI CRANBERRY SAUCE

1 pound ground raw turkey
¼ cup seasoned dry bread
crumbs
¼ cup thinly sliced green
onions
1 egg, slightly beaten
¼ teaspoon salt
¼ teaspoon pepper
1 tablespoon vegetable oil
⅔ cup whole-berry cranberry
sauce
⅓ cup HEINZ® Chili Sauce
2 tablespoons water
⅛ teaspoon ground cinnamon

Combine turkey, bread crumbs,
green onions, egg, salt and
pepper. Shape into 4 patties,
about ½ inch thick. Slowly sauté
patties in oil, about 4 to 5 minutes
per side or until no longer pink in
center. Stir in cranberry sauce,
chili sauce, water and cinnamon.
Simmer, uncovered, 1 minute.
Makes 4 servings

Chicken Paprika

CHICKEN SKILLET SUPPER

1 teaspoon salt
¼ teaspoon black pepper
¼ teaspoon ground paprika
⅛ teaspoon garlic powder
1 whole chicken (about
    3 pounds), cut into
    serving pieces
1 tablespoon vegetable oil
2 tablespoons water
1 medium onion, chopped
1 medium potato, peeled and
    cut into 2¼-inch strips
1 tablespoon slivered almonds
    (optional)
1 can (8 ounces) tomato sauce
1 cup chicken broth
1 teaspoon sugar
1 package (10 ounces) frozen
    French-cut green beans

Mix salt, pepper, paprika and garlic powder in small bowl; rub over chicken. Heat oil in large skillet over medium heat; add chicken, skin-side down. Cover and cook 10 minutes. Add water to chicken; cover and cook 30 minutes, turning chicken over every 10 minutes. Remove chicken from skillet; set aside.

Add onion, potato and almonds to pan juices; cook and stir until onion is tender, about 3 minutes. Add tomato sauce, broth and sugar; bring to a boil. Add beans and chicken; cover and cook until beans are tender, about 10 minutes. Serve hot.

Makes 4 to 6 servings

ROASTED CHICKEN WITH MAPLE GLAZE

1 (3-pound) broiler-fryer
1 small onion, cut into wedges
1 small orange, cut into
    wedges
¾ cup apple cider
¼ cup maple syrup
¾ teaspoon cornstarch
¼ teaspoon pumpkin pie spice

Preheat oven to 325°F. Remove giblets and neck from chicken; reserve for another use. Rinse chicken under cold water and pat dry with paper towels.

Place onion and orange wedges in cavity of chicken. Tie legs together with wet cotton string and place breast-side up on rack in shallow roasting pan coated with nonstick cooking spray. Insert meat thermometer into meaty part of thigh not touching bone.

Combine apple cider, maple syrup, cornstarch and pumpkin pie spice in small saucepan, stirring until cornstarch is dissolved. Bring to a boil over medium heat, stirring constantly; cook 1 minute. Brush apple cider mixture over chicken.

Bake chicken 1½ to 2 hours or until meat thermometer registers 180°F, basting frequently with remaining cider mixture.

Remove string from chicken; discard. Remove onion and orange wedges from chicken cavity; discard. Transfer chicken to serving platter. Let stand 10 minutes before carving.

Makes 4 servings

OLD–FASHIONED CHICKEN WITH DUMPLINGS

     3 to 3½ pounds chicken
         pieces
     3 tablespoons butter or
         margarine
     2 cans (about 14 ounces each)
         chicken broth
     3½ cups water
     1 teaspoon salt
     ¼ teaspoon white pepper
     2 large carrots, cut into 1-inch
         slices
     2 ribs celery, cut into 1-inch
         slices
     8 to 10 small boiling onions
     ¼ pound small mushrooms, cut
         into halves
         Parsley Dumplings (recipe
         follows)
     ½ cup frozen peas, thawed,
         drained

Brown chicken in melted butter in 6- to 8-quart Dutch oven over medium-high heat. Add broth, water, salt and pepper. Bring to a boil over high heat. Reduce heat to low. Cover; simmer 15 minutes. Add carrots, celery, onions and mushrooms. Simmer, covered, 40

minutes or until chicken and vegetables are tender.

Prepare Parsley Dumplings. When chicken is tender, skim fat from broth. Stir in peas. Drop dumpling mixture into broth, making 6 large or 12 small dumplings. Cover; simmer 15 to 20 minutes or until dumplings are firm to the touch and wooden pick inserted in center comes out clean.

Makes 6 servings

Parsley Dumplings: Sift 2 cups all-purpose flour, 4 teaspoons baking powder and ½ teaspoon salt into medium bowl. Cut in 5 tablespoons cold butter or margarine until mixture resembles coarse meal. Make a well in center; pour in 1 cup milk, all at once. Add 2 tablespoons chopped parsley; stir with fork until mixture forms a ball.

CASSEROLES

CREAMY CHICKEN AND PASTA WITH SPINACH

- 6 ounces uncooked egg noodles
- 1 tablespoon olive oil
- ¼ cup chopped onion
- ¼ cup chopped red bell pepper
- 1 package (10 ounces) frozen spinach, thawed and drained
- 2 boneless skinless chicken breast halves (¾ pound), cooked and cut into 1-inch pieces
- 1 can (4 ounces) sliced mushrooms, drained
- 2 cups (8 ounces) shredded Swiss cheese
- 1 container (8 ounces) sour cream
- ¾ cup half-and-half
- 2 eggs, slightly beaten
- ½ teaspoon salt
  Red onion and fresh spinach for garnish

Preheat oven to 350°F. Prepare egg noodles according to package directions; set aside.

Heat oil in large skillet over medium-high heat. Add onion and bell pepper; cook and stir 2 minutes or until onion is tender. Add spinach, chicken, mushrooms and cooked noodles; stir to combine.

Combine cheese, sour cream, half-and-half, eggs and salt in medium bowl; blend well.

Add cheese mixture to chicken mixture; stir to combine. Pour into 13×9-inch baking dish coated with nonstick cooking spray. Bake, covered, 30 to 35 minutes or until heated through. Garnish with red onion and fresh spinach, if desired.   *Makes 8 servings*

Creamy Chicken and Pasta with Spinach

BISCUIT–TOPPED HEARTY STEAK PIE

1½ pounds top round steak,
    cooked and cut into
    1-inch cubes
1 package (9 ounces) frozen
    baby carrots
1 package (9 ounces) frozen
    peas and pearl onions
1 large baking potato, cooked
    and cut into ½-inch
    pieces
1 jar (18 ounces) home-style
    brown gravy
½ teaspoon dried thyme leaves
½ teaspoon black pepper
1 can (10 ounces) refrigerated
    flaky buttermilk biscuits

Preheat oven to 375°F. Spray
2-quart square casserole with
nonstick cooking spray.

Combine steak, frozen vegetables
and potato in prepared dish. Stir
in gravy, thyme and pepper.

Bake, uncovered, 40 minutes.
Remove from oven. *Increase oven
temperature to 400°F.* Top with
biscuits and bake 8 to 10 minutes
or until biscuits are golden brown.

Makes 6 servings

OVEN CHICKEN & RICE

1 package (4.3 ounces)
    RICE-A-RONI® Long Grain
    & Wild Rice Pilaf
4 bone-in chicken breast
    halves
½ teaspoon dried thyme leaves
    or dried basil leaves
¼ teaspoon garlic powder
1 tablespoon margarine or
    butter, melted
½ teaspoon paprika
1 cup chopped tomato or red
    bell pepper

1. Heat oven to 375°F. In 11×7-
inch glass baking dish or 1½-quart
casserole, combine 1¼ cups
water, rice and contents of
seasoning packet; mix well.

2. Place chicken over rice.
Sprinkle evenly with thyme and
garlic powder. Brush with
margarine; sprinkle with paprika.

3. Cover with foil; bake 45
minutes. Stir in tomato. Bake,
uncovered, 15 minutes or until
liquid is absorbed and chicken is
no longer pink inside.

Makes 4 servings

Biscuit-Topped Hearty Steak Pie

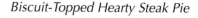

COUNTRY CHICKEN POT PIE

2 tablespoons butter or margarine
¾ pound boneless skinless chicken breasts, cut into 1-inch pieces
¾ teaspoon salt
8 ounces fresh green beans, cut into 1-inch pieces (2 cups)
½ cup chopped red bell pepper
½ cup thinly sliced celery
3 tablespoons all-purpose flour
½ cup chicken broth
½ cup half-and-half
1 teaspoon dried thyme leaves
½ teaspoon rubbed sage
1 cup frozen pearl onions
½ cup frozen corn
Pastry for single-crust 10-inch pie

Preheat oven to 425°F. Spray 10-inch deep-dish pie plate with nonstick cooking spray.

Melt margarine in large deep skillet over medium-high heat. Add chicken; cook and stir 3 minutes or until no longer pink in centers. Sprinkle with salt. Add beans, bell pepper and celery; cook and stir 3 minutes.

Sprinkle flour evenly over chicken and vegetables; cook and stir 1 minute. Stir in broth, half-and-half, thyme and sage; bring to a boil over high heat. Reduce heat to low and simmer 3 minutes or until sauce is very thick. Stir in onions and corn. Return to a simmer; cook and stir 1 minute.

Transfer mixture to prepared pie plate. Place pie crust over chicken mixture; turn edge under and crimp to seal. Cut 4 slits in pie crust to allow steam to escape.

Bake 20 minutes or until crust is light golden brown and mixture is hot and bubbly. Let stand 5 minutes before serving.

Makes 6 servings

TIP

For a decorative touch, make cutouts in the crust before placing it over the chicken mixture. Use a tiny cookie cutter or make simple cutouts with the tip of a paring knife.

Country Chicken Pot Pie

COUNTRY SAUSAGE MACARONI AND CHEESE

1 pound BOB EVANS® Special Seasonings Roll Sausage
1½ cups milk
12 ounces pasteurized processed Cheddar cheese, cut into cubes
½ cup Dijon mustard
1 cup diced fresh or drained canned tomatoes
1 cup sliced mushrooms
⅓ cup sliced green onions
⅛ teaspoon cayenne pepper
12 ounces uncooked elbow macaroni
2 tablespoons grated Parmesan cheese

Preheat oven to 350°F. Crumble and cook sausage in medium skillet until browned. Drain on paper towels. Combine milk, cheese and mustard in medium saucepan; cook and stir over low heat until cheese melts and mixture is smooth. Stir in sausage, tomatoes, mushrooms, green onions and cayenne pepper. Remove from heat.

Cook macaroni according to package directions; drain. Combine hot macaroni and cheese mixture in large bowl; toss until well coated. Spoon into greased 2-quart casserole dish. Cover and bake 15 to 20 minutes. Stir; sprinkle with Parmesan cheese. Bake, uncovered, 5 minutes more. Let stand 10 minutes before serving. Refrigerate leftovers.

Makes 6 to 8 servings

PORK CHOPS AND YAMS

4 pork chops (½ inch thick)
2 tablespoons oil
2 (16-ounce) cans yams or sweet potatoes, drained
¾ cup SMUCKER'S® Sweet Orange Marmalade or Apricot Preserves
½ large green bell pepper, cut into strips
2 tablespoons minced onion

Brown pork chops in oil over medium heat.

Place yams in 1½-quart casserole. Stir in marmalade, bell pepper and onion. Layer pork chops over yam mixture. Cover and bake at 350°F for 30 minutes or until pork chops are tender.

Makes 4 servings

Country Sausage Macaroni and Cheese

TURKEY & GREEN BEAN CASSEROLE

¼ cup slivered almonds
1 package (7 ounces) herb-seasoned stuffing cubes
¾ cup reduced-sodium chicken broth
1 can (10¾ ounces) condensed cream of mushroom soup, undiluted
¼ cup milk or half-and-half
¼ teaspoon black pepper
1 package (10 ounces) frozen French-style green beans, thawed and drained
2 cups (½-inch-thick) deli turkey breast or cooked turkey or chicken, cubed

Preheat oven to 350°F. Spray 11×7-inch baking dish with nonstick cooking spray.

Spread almonds in single layer on baking sheet. Bake 5 minutes or until golden brown, stirring frequently. Set aside.

Arrange stuffing cubes in prepared dish; drizzle with broth. Stir to coat bread cubes with broth.

Combine soup, milk and pepper in large bowl. Add green beans and turkey; stir until combined. Spoon over stuffing cubes; top with almonds.

Bake, uncovered, 30 to 35 minutes or until heated through.
Makes 4 servings

PENNSYLVANIA DUTCH CHICKEN BAKE

1 package (about 1¾ pounds) PERDUE® Fresh Skinless Chicken Thighs
Salt and pepper to taste
1 to 2 tablespoons canola oil
1 can (14 to 16 ounces) sauerkraut, undrained
1 can (14 to 15 ounces) whole onions, drained
1 tart red apple, unpeeled and sliced
6 to 8 dried whole apricots
½ cup raisins
¼ cup brown sugar, or to taste

Preheat oven to 350°F. Season thighs with salt and pepper. In large nonstick skillet over medium-high heat, heat oil. Cook thighs 6 to 8 minutes per side until browned. Meanwhile, in 12×9-inch shallow baking dish, mix sauerkraut, onions, apple, apricots, raisins and brown sugar until blended. Arrange thighs in sauerkraut mixture. Cover and bake 30 to 40 minutes or until chicken is cooked through and a meat thermometer inserted in thickest part of thigh registers 180°F. *Makes 6 servings*

Tip: If desired, substitute other fresh or dried fruit in this recipe, such as pears or pitted prunes.

Turkey & Green Bean Casserole

SMOKED SAUSAGE AND SAUERKRAUT CASSEROLE

6 fully cooked smoked sausage links, such as German or Polish sausage (about 1½ pounds), cut into thirds
¼ cup packed brown sugar
2 tablespoons country-style Dijon mustard or German-style mustard
1 teaspoon caraway seed
½ teaspoon dill weed
1 jar (32 ounces) sauerkraut, drained
1 green bell pepper, diced
½ cup (2 ounces) shredded Swiss cheese

1. Place sausage in large skillet with ⅓ cup water. Cover; bring to a boil over medium heat. Reduce heat to low; simmer, covered, 10 minutes. Uncover and simmer until water evaporates and sausages brown lightly.

2. While sausage is cooking, combine sugar, mustard, caraway and dill in medium saucepan; stir until blended. Add sauerkraut and bell pepper; stir until well mixed. Cook, covered, over medium heat 10 minutes or until very hot.

3. Spoon sauerkraut into microwavable 3-quart casserole; top with cheese. Place sausage into sauerkraut; cover. Microwave at HIGH 30 seconds or until cheese melts. *Makes 6 servings*

CAMPBELL'S® BAKED MACARONI & CHEESE

1 can (10¾ ounces) CAMPBELL'S® Condensed Cheddar Cheese Soup
½ soup can milk
⅛ teaspoon pepper
2 cups hot cooked corkscrew *or* medium shell macaroni (about 1½ cups uncooked)
1 tablespoon dry bread crumbs
2 teaspoons margarine *or* butter, melted

1. In 1-quart casserole mix soup, milk, pepper and macaroni.

2. Mix bread crumbs with margarine and sprinkle over macaroni mixture.

3. Bake at 400°F. for 20 minutes or until hot. *Makes 4 servings*

To Double Recipe: Double all ingredients, except increase margarine to 1 tablespoon, use 2-quart casserole and increase baking time to 25 minutes.

Prep Time: 20 minutes
Cook Time: 20 minutes

Smoked Sausage and Sauerkraut Casserole

SAVORY CHICKEN & BISCUITS

- **2 tablespoons olive or vegetable oil**
- **1 pound boneless skinless chicken breasts, cut into 1-inch pieces (about 2 cups)**
- **1 medium onion, chopped**
- **1 cup thinly sliced carrots**
- **1 cup thinly sliced celery**
- **1 envelope LIPTON® RECIPE SECRETS® Savory Herb with Garlic Soup Mix***
- **1 cup milk**
- **1 package (10 ounces) refrigerated flaky buttermilk biscuits**

Also terrific with LIPTON® RECIPE SECRETS® Golden Onion.

Preheat oven to 400°F.

In 12-inch skillet, heat oil over medium-high heat and cook chicken, stirring occasionally, 5 minutes or until almost done. Stir in onion, carrots and celery; cook, stirring occasionally, 3 minutes. Stir in savory herb with garlic soup mix blended with milk. Bring to the boiling point over medium-high heat, stirring occasionally; cook 1 minute. Turn into lightly greased 2-quart casserole; arrange biscuits on top of chicken mixture with edges touching. Bake 10 minutes or until biscuits are golden brown.

Makes about 4 servings

GREEN BEANS AND HAM

- **2 cups cubed cooked ham**
- **1 can (10 ounces) cream of mushroom soup**
- **½ cup 1% milk**
- **1 bag (16 ounces) BIRDS EYE® frozen Cut Green Beans**
- **1 can (2.8 ounces) French fried onions**

• In microwave-safe casserole dish, mix ham, soup, milk and green beans.

• Cover and microwave on HIGH 10 to 12 minutes or until well heated, stirring halfway through cook time. Uncover; sprinkle with fried onions.

• Microwave, uncovered, 3 to 5 minutes. Serve hot.

Makes 6 servings

Prep Time: 5 minutes
Cook Time: 15 minutes

Savory Chicken & Biscuits

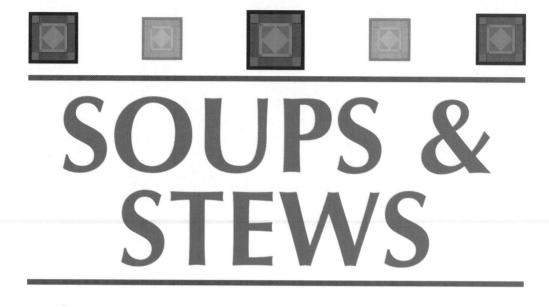

SOUPS & STEWS

OLD-FASHIONED BEEF STEW

  1 tablespoon CRISCO® Oil*
1¼ pounds boneless beef round
      steak, trimmed and cut
      into 1-inch cubes
2¾ cups water, divided
  1 teaspoon Worcestershire
      sauce
  2 bay leaves
  1 clove garlic, minced
  ½ teaspoon paprika
  ¼ teaspoon pepper
  8 medium carrots, quartered
  8 small potatoes, peeled and
      quartered
  4 small onions, quartered
  1 package (9 ounces) frozen
      cut green beans
  1 tablespoon cornstarch
    Salt (optional)

Any other Crisco® Oil can be substituted.

1. Heat oil in Dutch oven on medium-high heat. Add beef. Cook and stir until browned. Add 1½ cups water, Worcestershire sauce, bay leaves, garlic, paprika and pepper. Bring to a boil. Reduce heat to low. Cover. Simmer 1 hour 15 minutes, stirring occasionally. Remove and discard bay leaves.

2. Add carrots, potatoes and onions. Cover. Simmer 30 to 45 minutes or until vegetables are almost tender. Add beans. Simmer 5 minutes or until tender. Remove from heat. Add 1 cup water to Dutch oven.

3. Combine remaining ¼ cup water and cornstarch in small bowl. Stir well. Stir into ingredients in Dutch oven. Return to low heat. Cook and stir until thickened. Season with salt, if desired. *Makes 8 servings*

Old-Fashioned Beef Stew

COUNTRY BEAN SOUP

1¼ cups dried navy beans or
   lima beans, rinsed and
   drained
4 ounces salt pork or fully
   cooked ham, chopped
¼ cup chopped onion
½ teaspoon dried oregano
   leaves
¼ teaspoon salt
¼ teaspoon ground ginger
¼ teaspoon dried sage
¼ teaspoon ground black
   pepper
2 cups fat-free (skim) milk
2 tablespoons butter

1. Place navy beans in large saucepan; add enough water to cover beans. Bring to a boil; reduce heat and simmer 2 minutes. Remove from heat; cover and let stand for 1 hour. (Or, cover beans with water and soak overnight.)

2. Drain beans and return to saucepan. Stir in 2½ cups water, salt pork, onion, oregano, salt, ginger, sage and pepper. Bring to a boil; reduce heat. Cover and simmer 2 to 2½ hours or until beans are tender. (If necessary, add more water during cooking.) Add milk and butter, stirring until mixture is heated through and butter is melted. Season with additional salt and pepper, if desired.   *Makes 6 servings*

SAVORY PEA SOUP WITH SAUSAGE

8 ounces smoked sausage, cut
   lengthwise into halves,
   then cut into ½-inch
   pieces
2 cans (14½ ounces each)
   reduced-sodium chicken
   broth
1 package (16 ounces) dried
   split peas, sorted and
   rinsed
3 medium carrots, sliced
2 ribs celery, sliced
1 medium onion, chopped
¾ teaspoon dried marjoram
   leaves
1 bay leaf

SLOW COOKER DIRECTIONS
Heat small skillet over medium heat. Add sausage; cook 5 to 8 minutes or until browned. Drain well. Combine sausage and remaining ingredients in slow cooker. Cover and cook on LOW 4 to 5 hours or until peas are tender. Turn off heat. Remove and discard bay leaf. Cover and let stand 15 minutes to thicken.
                Makes 6 servings

Country Bean Soup

PORK AND VEGETABLE STEW WITH NOODLES

1 pound lean boneless pork
2 tablespoons vegetable oil
3 cups canned beef broth
3 tablespoons chopped fresh parsley, divided
1 can (14½ ounces) stewed tomatoes
1 large carrot, sliced
3 green onions, sliced
2 teaspoons Dijon mustard
¼ teaspoon rubbed sage
⅛ teaspoon black pepper
3 cups uncooked noodles
1 teaspoon butter or margarine
2 tablespoons all-purpose flour
⅓ cup cold water
Apples and parsley for garnish

Cut pork into ¾-inch cubes. Heat oil in large saucepan over medium-high heat. Add meat; brown, stirring frequently. Carefully add beef broth. Stir in 1 tablespoon chopped parsley, tomatoes, carrot, onions, mustard, sage and pepper. Bring to a boil over high heat. Reduce heat to medium-low; simmer, uncovered, 30 minutes.

Meanwhile, cook noodles according to package directions; drain. Add remaining 2 tablespoons chopped parsley and butter; toss lightly. Keep warm until ready to serve.

Stir flour into cold water in cup until smooth. Stir into stew. Cook and stir over medium heat until slightly thickened. To serve, spoon noodles onto each plate. Ladle stew over noodles. Garnish, if desired.   *Makes 4 servings*

HEARTY ONE–POT CHICKEN STEW

12 boneless, skinless chicken tenderloins, cut into 1-inch pieces
1 box UNCLE BEN'S® Red Beans & Rice
2¼ cups water
1 can (14½ ounces) diced tomatoes, undrained
3 red potatoes, unpeeled, cut into 1-inch pieces
2 carrots, sliced ½ inch thick
1 onion, cut into 1-inch pieces

1. In large saucepan, combine chicken, beans & rice, contents of seasoning packet, water, tomatoes, potatoes, carrots and onion. Bring to a boil. Cover; reduce heat and simmer 20 minutes or until vegetables are tender.

Makes 4 servings

Pork and Vegetable Stew with Noodles

CHICKEN AND HOMEMADE NOODLE SOUP

$^3/_4$ cup all-purpose flour
2 teaspoons finely chopped fresh thyme *or* $^1/_2$ teaspoon dried thyme, divided
$^1/_4$ teaspoon salt
1 egg yolk, beaten
3 tablespoons cold water
1 pound boneless skinless chicken thighs, cut into $^1/_2$- to $^3/_4$-inch pieces
2 cups cold water
5 cups chicken broth
1 medium onion, chopped
1 medium carrot, thinly sliced
$^3/_4$ cup frozen peas
Chopped fresh parsley

To prepare noodles, stir together flour, 1 teaspoon thyme and salt in small bowl. Add egg yolk and 3 tablespoons water. Mix well. Shape into small ball. Place dough on lightly floured surface; flatten slightly. Knead 5 minutes or until dough is smooth and elastic, adding more flour to prevent sticking if necessary. Cover with plastic wrap. Let stand 15 minutes.

Roll out dough to $^1/_8$-inch thickness or thinner on lightly floured surface with lightly floured rolling pin. Let rolled out dough stand about 30 minutes to dry slightly. Cut into $^1/_4$-inch-wide strips. Cut pieces $1^1/_2$ to 2 inches long.

Combine chicken and 2 cups water in medium saucepan. Bring to a boil over high heat. Reduce heat to medium-low; cover and simmer 5 minutes. Drain and rinse chicken; set aside. Combine chicken broth, onion, carrot and remaining 1 teaspoon thyme in 5-quart Dutch oven or large saucepan. Bring to a boil over high heat. Add noodles. Reduce heat to medium-low; simmer, uncovered, 8 minutes or until noodles are done. Stir in chicken and peas. Bring soup just to a boil. Sprinkle parsley over each serving.   *Makes 4 servings*

TIP

To prevent the noodles from sticking together, be sure the broth mixture maintains a constant boil during cooking.

Chicken and Homemade Noodle Soup

PORK AND CABBAGE SOUP

½ pound pork loin
2 strips bacon
1 medium onion, chopped
2 cups canned beef broth
2 cups canned chicken broth
1 can (28 ounces) tomatoes, cut-up, drained
2 medium carrots, sliced
¾ teaspoon dried marjoram leaves
1 bay leaf
⅛ teaspoon ground black pepper
¼ medium cabbage, chopped
2 tablespoons chopped fresh parsley
Additional chopped fresh parsley

1. Cut pork into ½-inch cubes. Finely chop bacon. Cook and stir onion, pork and bacon in 5-quart Dutch oven over medium heat until meat loses its pink color and onion is slightly tender. Remove from heat. Drain fat.

2. Stir in beef and chicken broth, tomatoes, carrots, marjoram, bay leaf and pepper. Bring to a boil over high heat. Reduce heat to medium-low; simmer, uncovered, about 30 minutes. Discard bay leaf. Skim off fat.

3. Stir cabbage into soup. Bring to a boil over high heat. Reduce heat to medium-low; simmer, uncovered, about 15 minutes or until cabbage is tender.

4. Remove soup from heat; stir in 2 tablespoons parsley. Ladle into bowls. Garnish each serving with additional parsley.

Makes 6 servings

HEARTY CHICKEN AND RICE SOUP

10 cups chicken broth
1 medium onion, chopped
1 cup sliced celery
1 cup sliced carrots
¼ cup snipped parsley
½ teaspoon cracked black pepper
½ teaspoon dried thyme leaves
1 bay leaf
1½ cups chicken cubes (about ¾ pound)
2 cups cooked rice
2 tablespoons lime juice
Lime slices for garnish

Combine broth, onion, celery, carrots, parsley, pepper, thyme and bay leaf in Dutch oven. Bring to a boil; stir once or twice. Reduce heat; simmer, uncovered, 10 to 15 minutes. Add chicken; simmer, uncovered, 5 to 10 minutes or until chicken is no longer pink in center. Remove and discard bay leaf. Stir in rice and lime juice just before serving. Garnish with lime slices.

Makes 8 servings

Favorite recipe from **USA Rice Federation**

Pork and Cabbage Soup

CHICKEN AND DUMPLINGS STEW

STEW

    2 cans (about 14 ounces each) fat-free reduced-sodium chicken broth
    1 pound boneless skinless chicken breast halves, cut into bite-sized pieces
    1 cup diagonally sliced carrots
    ¾ cup diagonally sliced celery
    1 onion, halved and cut into small wedges
    3 small new potatoes, unpeeled and cubed
    ½ teaspoon dried rosemary
    ¼ teaspoon pepper
    1 can (14½ ounces) diced tomatoes, drained *or* 1½ cups diced fresh tomatoes
    3 tablespoons all-purpose flour blended with ⅓ cup water

DUMPLINGS

    ¾ cup all-purpose flour
    1 teaspoon baking powder
    ¼ teaspoon onion powder
    ¼ teaspoon salt
    1 to 2 tablespoons finely chopped parsley
    ¼ cup cholesterol-free egg substitute
    ¼ cup low-fat (1%) milk
    1 tablespoon vegetable oil

1. For stew, bring broth to a boil in Dutch oven; add chicken. Cover; simmer 3 minutes. Add carrots, celery, onion, potatoes, rosemary and pepper. Cover; simmer 10 minutes. Reduce heat; stir in tomatoes and flour mixture. Cook and stir until broth thickens.

2. For dumplings combine ¾ cup flour, baking powder, onion powder and salt in medium bowl; blend in parsley. Combine egg substitute, milk and oil in small bowl; stir into flour mixture. *Do not overmix.*

3. Return broth mixture to a boil. Drop 8 tablespoons of dumpling batter into broth; cover tightly. Reduce heat; simmer 18 to 20 minutes. *Do not lift lid.* Dumplings are done when toothpick inserted in centers comes out clean.

Makes 4 servings

TIP

For best results when cooking dumplings, the broth mixture should simmer gently.

Chicken and Dumplings Stew

SIDE DISHES

IOWA CORN PUDDING

½ cup egg substitute or 2 large
  eggs
2 large egg whites
3 tablespoons all-purpose
  flour
1 tablespoon sugar
½ teaspoon freshly ground
  black pepper
1 can (16½ ounces) cream-
  style corn
2 cups fresh corn kernels or
  frozen corn, thawed and
  drained
1 cup (4 ounces) shredded
  ALPINE LACE® American
  Flavor Pasteurized Process
  Cheese Product
½ cup finely chopped red bell
  pepper
⅓ cup 2% low fat milk
1 tablespoon unsalted butter
  substitute
¼ teaspoon paprika
  Sprigs of fresh parsley

1. Preheat the oven to 350°F.
Spray an 8-inch round baking dish
with nonstick cooking spray. (A
deep-dish pie plate works well.)
Place in the oven to heat.

2. Meanwhile, in a large bowl,
using an electric mixer set on
high, beat the egg substitute (or
the whole eggs) and egg whites
with the flour, sugar and black
pepper until smooth. Stir in the
cream-style corn, corn kernels,
cheese, bell pepper and milk.
Pour into the hot baking dish.

3. Dot with the butter and sprinkle
with the paprika. Bake,
uncovered, for 55 minutes or until
set. Let stand for 15 minutes
before serving. Garnish with the
parsley.   *Makes 6 servings*

Iowa Corn Pudding

ROASTED POTATOES AND PEARL ONIONS

3 pounds red potatoes, well-scrubbed, cut into 1½-inch cubes
1 package (10 ounces) pearl onions, peeled
2 tablespoons olive oil
2 teaspoons dried basil leaves or thyme leaves
1 teaspoon paprika
¾ teaspoon dried rosemary, crushed
¾ teaspoon salt
¾ teaspoon ground black pepper

1. Preheat oven to 400°F. Spray large shallow roasting pan (do not use glass or potatoes will not brown) with nonstick cooking spray.

2. Add potatoes and onions to pan; drizzle with oil. Combine basil, paprika, rosemary, salt and pepper in small bowl; mix well. Sprinkle over potatoes and onions; toss well to coat lightly with oil and seasonings.

3. Bake 20 minutes; toss well. Continue baking 15 to 20 minutes or until potatoes are browned and tender.   *Makes 8 servings*

BAKED SQUASH

2 medium-sized acorn squash
2 tart red apples, diced
½ cup chopped nuts
½ cup SMUCKER'S® Apple Jelly
¼ cup butter or margarine, softened

Cut squash in half crosswise or lengthwise; scoop out centers. Place in baking pan. Combine apples, nuts, jelly and butter. Fill squash with mixture. Pour a small amount of boiling water in bottom of pan around squash. Cover pan with foil.

Bake at 400°F for 45 to 60 minutes or until fork-tender. Remove foil during last 5 minutes of baking.   *Makes 4 servings*

 **TIP**

To peel pearl onions, drop them into boiling water for about two minutes. Drain and plunge them into cold water. Cut off the stem end and squeeze the onions to separate them from their skins.

Roasted Potatoes and Pearl Onions

CAMPBELL'S® CREAMED ONION BAKE

4 tablespoons margarine *or* butter
1½ cups PEPPERIDGE FARM® Corn Bread Stuffing
2 tablespoons chopped fresh parsley *or* 2 teaspoons dried parsley flakes
3 large onions, cut in half and sliced (about 3 cups)
1 can (10¾ ounces) CAMPBELL'S® Condensed Cream of Mushroom Soup *or* 98% Fat Free Cream of Mushroom Soup
¼ cup milk
1 cup frozen peas
1 cup shredded Cheddar cheese (4 ounces)

1. Melt **2 tablespoons** margarine and mix with stuffing and parsley. Set aside.

2. In medium skillet over medium heat, heat remaining margarine. Add onions and cook until tender.

3. Stir in soup, milk and peas. Spoon into 2-quart shallow baking dish. Sprinkle cheese and stuffing mixture over soup mixture.

4. Bake at 350°F. for 30 minutes or until hot.   *Makes 6 servings*

Prep Time: 15 minutes
Cook Time: 30 minutes

APPLE & CARROT CASSEROLE

6 large carrots, sliced
4 large apples, peeled and sliced
5 tablespoons all-purpose flour
1 tablespoon packed brown sugar
½ teaspoon salt
½ teaspoon ground nutmeg
1 tablespoon margarine
½ cup orange juice

Preheat oven to 350°F. Cook carrots in large saucepan in boiling water 5 minutes; drain. Layer carrots and apples in large casserole. Combine flour, sugar, salt and nutmeg; sprinkle over top. Dot with margarine; pour orange juice over flour mixture. Bake 30 minutes or until carrots are tender.   *Makes 6 servings*

TIP

For this casserole, use Golden Delicious, Granny Smith or Jonathan apples.

Apple & Carrot Casserole

APRICOT–GLAZED BEETS

1 pound fresh beets
1 cup apricot nectar
1 tablespoon cornstarch
2 tablespoons cider vinegar or red wine vinegar
8 dried apricot halves, cut into strips
¼ teaspoon salt
Additional apricot halves (optional)

Cut tops off beets, leaving at least 1 inch of stems (do not trim root ends). Scrub beets under running water with soft vegetable brush, being careful not to break skins. Place beets in medium saucepan; cover with water. Bring to a boil over high heat; reduce heat to medium. Cover and simmer about 20 minutes or until just barely firm when pierced with fork and skins rub off easily. Transfer to plate; cool. Rinse pan.

Combine apricot nectar and cornstarch in same saucepan; stir in vinegar. Add apricot strips and salt. Cook over medium heat until mixture thickens.

Cut roots and stems from beets on plate.* Peel and cut beets into ¼-inch slices. Add beet slices to apricot mixture; toss to coat. Transfer to serving dish. Serve with apricot halves.

Makes 4 servings

*Do not cut beets on cutting board; the juice will stain the board.

RED CABBAGE WITH APPLES

1 small head red cabbage, shredded
2 large apples, peeled and thinly sliced
½ cup sliced onion
½ cup unsweetened apple juice
¼ cup lemon juice
2 tablespoons raisins
2 tablespoons brown sugar
Salt and pepper to taste (optional)

Combine cabbage, apples, onion, apple juice, lemon juice, raisins and brown sugar in large nonstick saucepan. Simmer, covered, 30 minutes. Season with salt and pepper. *Makes 8 servings*

Apricot-Glazed Beets

ROASTED SAVORY POTATOES

½ cup mayonnaise*
1 teaspoon LAWRY'S® Garlic
  Powder with Parsley
½ to ¾ teaspoon LAWRY'S®
  Seasoned Pepper
½ teaspoon LAWRY'S®
  Seasoned Salt
¼ teaspoon dried rosemary,
  crushed (optional)
2 medium russet potatoes, cut
  into ¼-inch-thick slices
½ cup sliced green onion
¼ cup (1 ounce) grated
  Parmesan cheese

Reduced calorie mayonnaise works great too!

In 9-inch square glass baking dish, combine mayonnaise, seasonings and rosemary. Add potatoes and onion; stir gently to coat. Sprinkle with cheese. Cover. Bake in 350°F oven 45 minutes; uncover. Bake 5 minutes longer to brown.

Makes 4 to 6 servings

Serving Suggestion: Serve with grilled meat, fish or poultry.

Hint: For a hint of mustard try this idea: Reduce mayonnaise to ¼ cup and add ¼ cup Dijon-style mustard. Continue as directed.

FRESH & FANCY CUCUMBER SALAD

2 medium cucumbers,
  unpeeled (about 1½ to
  1¾ pounds)
⅔ cup seasoned rice vinegar
⅓ cup WESSON® Canola Oil
1½ tablespoons chopped fresh
  dill *or* 1 teaspoon dried
  dill weed
½ teaspoon salt
½ teaspoon sugar
  Pinch pepper
1½ cups red onion wedges
  (⅛ inch thick)

Slightly piercing cucumber skins, run fork tines down length of cucumbers on *all* sides; thinly slice. In medium bowl, combine vinegar, Wesson® Oil, dill, salt, sugar and pepper; mix until sugar is dissolved. Toss in cucumbers and onions; mix until vegetables are well coated with dressing. Refrigerate 15 minutes. Toss salad before serving. Serve with slotted spoon. *Makes 4 to 6 servings*

Fresh & Fancy Cucumber Salad

HOT GERMAN POTATO SALAD

1½ pounds new or boiling-type potatoes, cut into ¾-inch cubes
1⅓ cups water, divided
½ teaspoon salt
½ pound bacon, cut crosswise into thin strips
2 tablespoons cider vinegar
4 teaspoons sugar
1 tablespoon FRENCH'S® Worcestershire Sauce
2 teaspoons cornstarch
¼ teaspoon ground black pepper
1⅓ cups FRENCH'S® French Fried Onions, divided
1 cup chopped green bell pepper
1 cup chopped celery
¼ cup chopped pimento

Place potatoes, 1 cup water and salt in 3-quart microwave-safe dish. Cover and microwave on HIGH 15 minutes or until potatoes are tender, stirring once. Drain in colander; set aside.

Place bacon in same dish. Microwave, uncovered, on HIGH 5 minutes or until bacon is crisp, stirring once. Remove bacon with slotted spoon; set aside. Pour off all but ¼ cup bacon drippings. Stir in remaining ⅓ cup water, vinegar, sugar, Worcestershire, cornstarch and black pepper. Microwave, uncovered, on HIGH 1 to 2 minutes or until dressing has thickened, stirring once.

Return potatoes to dish. Add ⅔ cup French Fried Onions, bell pepper, celery, pimento and reserved bacon; toss well to coat evenly. Microwave, uncovered, on HIGH 2 minutes. Stir. Sprinkle with remaining ⅔ cup onions. Microwave on HIGH 1 minute or until onions are golden. Serve warm.

Makes 6 side-dish servings

Prep Time: 20 minutes
Cook Time: 25 minutes

CLASSIC WALDORF SALAD

½ cup HELLMANN'S® or BEST FOODS® Mayonnaise
1 tablespoon sugar
1 tablespoon lemon juice
⅛ teaspoon salt
3 medium-size red apples, cored and diced
1 cup sliced celery
½ cup chopped walnuts

1. In medium bowl combine mayonnaise, sugar, lemon juice and salt.

2. Add apples and celery; toss to coat well. Cover; chill. Just before serving, sprinkle with walnuts.

Makes about 8 servings

SMUCKER'S® THREE BEAN SALAD WITH SWEET AND SOUR APRICOT DRESSING

½ cup SMUCKER'S® Apricot
    Preserves
¼ cup red wine vinegar
1 teaspoon celery seeds
1 (16-ounce) can kidney
    beans, rinsed and drained
1 cup cooked fresh or frozen
    green beans, cut into
    2-inch pieces
1 cup cooked fresh or frozen
    yellow wax beans, cut
    into 2-inch pieces
1 small red onion, thinly
    sliced
    Salt and pepper to taste

Combine Smucker's® Apricot
Preserves, vinegar and celery
seeds in medium salad bowl. Add
kidney beans, green and yellow
beans and onion. Toss well to
combine. Season with salt and
freshly ground pepper.

Makes 6 servings

CREAMY DIJON COLESLAW

½ cup GREY POUPON®
    COUNTRY DIJON®
    Mustard
½ cup prepared ranch, creamy
    Italian or blue cheese
    salad dressing
2 tablespoons chopped parsley
½ teaspoon celery seed
3 cups shredded green
    cabbage
2 cups shredded red cabbage
1 cup shredded carrots
½ cup chopped onion
⅓ cup chopped red bell
    pepper

In small bowl, blend mustard,
salad dressing, parsley and celery
seed; set aside.

In large bowl, combine green and
red cabbages, carrots, onion and
bell pepper. Add mustard mixture,
tossing to coat well. Chill at least
1 hour before serving.

Makes about 5 cups

 TIP

Choose green or yellow wax beans with crisp, unblemished pods. Slenderness is an indication of tenderness.

BREADS

APPLE BUTTER SPICE MUFFINS

½ cup sugar
1 teaspoon ground cinnamon
¼ teaspoon ground nutmeg
⅛ teaspoon ground allspice
½ cup pecans or walnuts, chopped
2 cups all-purpose flour
2 teaspoons baking powder
¼ teaspoon salt
1 cup milk
¼ cup vegetable oil
1 egg
¼ cup apple butter

1. Preheat oven to 400°F. Grease or paper-line 12 (2½-inch) muffin cups.

2. Combine sugar, cinnamon, nutmeg and allspice in large bowl. Toss 2 tablespoons sugar mixture with pecans in small bowl; set aside. Add flour, baking powder and salt to remaining sugar mixture.

3. Combine milk, oil and egg in medium bowl. Stir into flour mixture just until moistened.

4. Spoon 1 tablespoon batter into each prepared muffin cup. Spoon 1 teaspoon apple butter into each cup. Spoon remaining batter evenly over apple butter. Sprinkle reserved pecan mixture over each muffin. Bake 20 to 25 minutes or until golden brown and wooden toothpick inserted in center comes out clean. Immediately remove from pan; cool on wire rack 10 minutes. Serve warm or cold.

Makes 12 muffins

 **TIP**

Mix muffin batter just until dry ingredients are moistened; some lumps may remain. Overmixing will give muffins a tough texture.

Apple Butter Spice Muffins

CORN BREAD

1 cup all-purpose flour
1 cup yellow cornmeal
⅓ cup sugar
2 teaspoons baking powder
½ teaspoon salt
1 cup milk
⅓ cup vegetable oil
1 egg

1. Preheat oven to 400°F. Grease 8-inch square baking pan.

2. Combine flour, cornmeal, sugar, baking powder and salt in large bowl. Combine milk, oil and egg in small bowl until blended. Stir milk mixture into flour mixture just until moistened. Spread batter into prepared pan.

3. Bake 20 to 25 minutes or until golden brown and toothpick inserted in center comes out clean. Cut into squares. Serve warm. *Makes 9 servings*

Corn Muffins: Preheat oven to 400°F. Prepare batter as directed except spoon batter into 12 (2½-inch) greased or paper-lined muffin cups. Bake 20 minutes or until golden brown and toothpick inserted in center comes out clean. Remove from pan; cool on wire rack 10 minutes. Makes 12 muffins.

Corn Sticks: Prepare batter as directed above and bake in cast-iron corn stick pans following manufacturer's directions.

PLUM HONEY TEA BREAD

2 cups all-purpose flour
1 teaspoon baking powder
1 teaspoon baking soda
1 teaspoon ground cinnamon
½ teaspoon salt
¼ teaspoon ground nutmeg
¾ cup buttermilk
½ cup honey
2 tablespoons vegetable oil
1 egg, beaten
3 plums, pitted and chopped
½ cup chopped walnuts

Combine flour, baking powder, baking soda, cinnamon, salt and nutmeg in large bowl; mix well. Combine buttermilk, honey, oil and egg in small bowl; mix until blended. Stir buttermilk mixture into flour mixture until just moistened. Fold in plums and walnuts. Pour into greased 9×5×3-inch loaf pan. Bake at 325°F 50 to 55 minutes or until wooden pick inserted near center comes out clean. During baking, cover top with foil after 25 minutes to prevent overbrowning. *Makes 8 servings*

Favorite recipe from **National Honey Board**

Plum Honey Tea Bread

COUNTRY BUTTERMILK BISCUITS

2 cups all-purpose flour
1 tablespoon baking powder
2 teaspoons sugar
½ teaspoon baking soda
½ teaspoon salt
⅓ cup vegetable shortening
⅔ cup buttermilk*

Or, substitute soured fresh milk. To sour milk, place 2½ teaspoons lemon juice plus enough milk to equal ⅔ cup in 1-cup measure. Stir; let stand 5 minutes before using.

1. Preheat oven to 450°F.

2. Combine flour, baking powder, sugar, baking soda and salt in medium bowl. Cut in shortening with pastry blender or 2 knives until mixture resembles coarse crumbs. Make well in center of dry ingredients. Add buttermilk; stir until mixture forms soft dough that clings together and forms a ball.

3. Turn out dough onto well-floured surface. Knead dough gently 10 to 12 times. Roll or pat dough to ½-inch thickness. Cut out dough with floured 2½-inch biscuit cutter.

4. Place biscuits 2 inches apart on *ungreased* large baking sheet. Bake 8 to 10 minutes or until tops and bottoms are golden brown. Serve warm.

Makes about 9 biscuits

Drop Biscuits: Prepare Country Buttermilk Biscuits as directed in steps 1 through 2, except grease 2 small baking sheets and increase buttermilk to 1 cup. After adding buttermilk, stir batter with wooden spoon about 15 strokes. *Do not knead.* Drop dough by heaping tablespoonfuls, 1 inch apart, onto prepared baking sheets. Bake as directed in step 4. Makes about 18 biscuits.

Sour Cream Dill Biscuits: Prepare Country Buttermilk Biscuits as directed in steps 1 through 2, except omit buttermilk. Combine ½ cup sour cream, ⅓ cup milk and 1 tablespoon chopped fresh dill *or* 1 teaspoon dried dill weed in small bowl until well blended. Stir into dry ingredients and continue as directed in step 3. Makes about 9 biscuits.

Bacon 'n' Onion Biscuits: Prepare Country Buttermilk Biscuits as directed in steps 1 through 2, except add 4 slices crumbled cooked bacon (about ⅓ cup) and ⅓ cup chopped green onions (about 3 medium onions) to flour-shortening mixture before adding buttermilk. Continue as directed in step 3. Makes about 9 biscuits.

Country Buttermilk Biscuits

PINEAPPLE ALMOND DATE BREAD

1 cup DOLE® Sliced Almonds, divided
2 cups all-purpose flour
1 teaspoon baking powder
1 teaspoon baking soda
¼ teaspoon ground nutmeg
¾ cup sugar
½ cup margarine, softened
1 egg
1 can (8 ounces) DOLE® Crushed Pineapple
Grated peel from 1 DOLE® Orange (1 tablespoon)
1 cup DOLE® Chopped Dates

• Preheat oven to 350°F. Toast ¾ cup almonds; reserve remaining ¼ cup for topping.

• Combine flour, baking powder, baking soda and nutmeg in medium bowl.

• Beat sugar and margarine in bowl until fluffy. Blend in egg. Stir in undrained pineapple and orange peel. Beat in flour mixture until blended. Stir in toasted almonds and dates.

• Turn batter into well greased 9×5-inch loaf pan. Sprinkle remaining ¼ cup untoasted almonds on top. Bake 55 to 60 minutes or until toothpick inserted in center comes out clean. Cool in pan 10 minutes. Turn onto wire rack. *Makes 1 loaf*

Prep Time: 15 minutes
Bake Time: 60 minutes

MOLASSES BROWN BREAD

1 cup all-purpose flour
1 cup graham or rye flour
1 cup whole wheat flour
1 teaspoon baking soda
½ teaspoon salt
1 cup buttermilk
1 cup light molasses
½ cup golden or dark raisins
½ cup chopped walnuts or pecans
Reduced-fat or fat-free cream cheese (optional)

1. Preheat oven to 350°F. Combine all-purpose flour, graham flour, whole wheat flour, baking soda and salt in large bowl. Add buttermilk and molasses; mix well. Stir in raisins and nuts.

2. Spray 9×5-inch loaf pan with nonstick cooking spray. Spoon batter evenly into pan. Bake 50 to 55 minutes or until wooden pick inserted near center comes out clean.

3. Transfer pan to wire cooling rack; let stand 10 minutes. Turn bread out onto wire rack; cool completely. Cut into slices. Serve at room temperature with cream cheese, if desired.
Makes about 16 slices

Molasses Brown Bread

FARMER–STYLE SOUR CREAM BREAD

1 cup sour cream, at room temperature
3 tablespoons water
2½ to 3 cups all-purpose flour, divided
1 package active dry yeast
2 tablespoons sugar
1½ teaspoons salt
¼ teaspoon baking soda
Vegetable oil or nonstick cooking spray
1 tablespoon poppy or sesame seeds

Stir together sour cream and water in small saucepan. Heat over low heat until temperature reaches 120° to 130°F. *Do not boil.* Combine 2 cups flour, yeast, sugar, salt and baking soda in a large bowl. Spread sour cream mixture evenly over flour mixture with rubber spatula. Stir until well blended. Turn out dough onto lightly floured surface. Knead 5 minutes or until smooth and elastic, gradually adding remaining flour to prevent sticking, if necessary.

Grease large baking sheet. Shape dough into ball; place on prepared sheet. Flatten into 8-inch circle. Brush with oil. Sprinkle with poppy seeds. Invert large bowl over dough and let rise in warm place 1 hour or until doubled in bulk.

Preheat oven to 350°F. Bake 22 to 27 minutes or until golden brown. Remove immediately from baking sheet. Cool completely on wire rack.   *Makes 8 to 12 servings*

PEACH AND SAUSAGE WAFFLES

½ pound BOB EVANS® Original Recipe Roll Sausage
1 cup all-purpose flour
3 tablespoons sugar
2 teaspoons baking powder
2 eggs
2 cups milk
4 tablespoons melted butter
1 cup chopped, drained canned peaches

Preheat waffle iron. If preparing waffles in advance, preheat oven to 200°F. Crumble and cook sausage in medium skillet until browned; drain on paper towels. Whisk flour, sugar and baking powder in large bowl. Whisk eggs and milk in medium bowl until well blended. Pour liquid ingredients over dry ingredients; whisk until just combined. Stir in butter until blended. Stir in peaches and sausage. Lightly butter grids of waffle iron; add ½ cup batter to hot iron. Cook waffles according to manufacturer's instructions. Serve immediately.   *Makes 6 servings*

Farmer-Style Sour Cream Bread

BAKED DOUGHNUTS WITH CINNAMON GLAZE

5 to 5½ cups all-purpose flour, divided
⅔ cup granulated sugar
2 packages active dry yeast
1 teaspoon salt
1 teaspoon grated lemon peel
½ teaspoon ground nutmeg
2 cups milk, divided
½ cup butter
2 eggs
2 cups sifted powdered sugar
½ teaspoon ground cinnamon

1. Combine 2 cups flour, granulated sugar, yeast, salt, lemon peel and nutmeg in large bowl. Combine 1¾ cups milk and butter in 1-quart saucepan. Heat over low heat until mixture is 120° to 130°F. (Butter does not need to completely melt.) Gradually beat milk mixture into flour mixture with electric mixer at low speed. Increase speed to medium; beat 2 minutes.

2. Beat in eggs and 1 cup flour at low speed. Increase speed to medium; beat 2 minutes. Stir in enough additional flour, about 2 cups, to make soft dough. Cover with greased plastic wrap; refrigerate at least 2 hours or up to 24 hours.

3. Punch down dough. Turn out dough onto lightly floured surface. Knead dough about 1 minute or until dough is no longer sticky, adding remaining ½ cup flour to prevent sticking if necessary.

4. Grease 2 large baking sheets. Roll out dough to ½-inch thickness with lightly floured rolling pin. Cut dough with floured 2¾-inch doughnut cutter. Reroll scraps, reserving doughnut holes. Place doughnuts and holes 2 inches apart on prepared baking sheets. Cover with towels; let rise in warm place about 30 minutes or until doubled in bulk.

5. To prepare glaze, combine powdered sugar and cinnamon in small bowl. Stir in enough remaining milk, about ¼ cup, to thin glaze to desired consistency. Cover; set aside.

6. Preheat oven to 400°F. Place pieces of waxed paper under wire racks to keep counter clean. Bake doughnuts and holes 8 to 10 minutes or until golden brown. Remove from pan; cool on wire racks 5 minutes. Dip warm doughnuts into glaze. Place right side up on racks, allowing glaze to drip down sides. Serve warm.

Makes 2 dozen doughnuts and holes

Baked Doughnuts with Cinnamon Glaze

MAPLE–PUMPKIN–PECAN TWIST

1 can (15 ounces) pumpkin
1 cup water
½ cup vegetable shortening
7 to 8 cups all-purpose flour, divided
2 cups pecans, coarsely chopped
½ cup sugar
2 packages active dry yeast
2 teaspoons salt
2 large eggs
2 teaspoons maple flavoring, divided
2 cups powdered sugar
6 to 8 tablespoons milk

1. Heat pumpkin, water and shortening in medium saucepan over medium heat until shortening is melted and temperature reaches 120° to 130°F. Remove from heat.

2. Combine 4 cups flour, pecans, sugar, yeast and salt in large bowl. Add pumpkin mixture, eggs and 1 teaspoon maple flavoring; beat vigorously 2 minutes. Add remaining flour, ¼ cup at a time, until dough begins to pull away from sides of bowl. Turn out dough onto lightly floured work surface; flatten slightly. Knead 10 minutes or until smooth and elastic, adding flour if necessary to prevent sticking. Shape dough into ball. Place in large lightly oiled bowl; turn dough over once to oil surface. Cover with towel; let rise in warm place about 1 hour or until doubled in bulk.

3. Turn out dough onto lightly oiled work surface; divide into four pieces. Shape each piece into 24-inch-long rope. Lightly twist two of the ropes together. Tuck ends under loaf to prevent untwisting. Place on lightly oiled baking sheet. Repeat with remaining two ropes. Cover with towel; let rise in warm place 45 minutes.

4. Preheat oven to 375°F. Bake 25 minutes or until deep golden brown. Immediately remove bread from baking sheets and cool on wire rack 20 minutes.

5. Whisk powdered sugar, 6 tablespoons milk and remaining 1 teaspoon maple flavoring in medium bowl. If icing is too thick, add remaining milk, 1 teaspoon at a time, to reach desired consistency. Drizzle over loaves in zigzag pattern.

Makes 2 large twists

 **TIP**

To test if yeast dough has risen properly, lightly press two fingertips about one-half inch into the dough. The dough is ready if indentations remain when fingertips are removed.

Maple-Pumpkin-Pecan Twist

DESSERTS

APPLE CRANBERRY BUCKLE

6 medium Granny Smith apples, peeled, cored and thinly sliced
¾ cup dried cranberries or dried cherries
⅓ cup orange juice
⅔ cup packed light brown sugar
1½ cups plus 2 tablespoons all-purpose flour, divided
1¼ teaspoons ground cinnamon
¼ teaspoon ground cloves
¾ cup plus 1 teaspoon granulated sugar, divided
1½ teaspoons baking powder
1 egg
⅓ cup milk
¼ cup butter or margarine, melted
1 cup apple butter
2 tablespoons amaretto liqueur or apple juice
Mint leaves (optional)

Preheat oven to 375°F. Place apples and cranberries in 11×7-inch baking dish. Drizzle orange juice over fruit.

Combine brown sugar, 2 tablespoons flour, cinnamon and cloves in small bowl. Pour over apple mixture; toss to coat.

Combine remaining 1½ cups flour, ¾ cup granulated sugar and baking powder in medium bowl. Add egg, milk and margarine; stir with mixing spoon to blend. Drop tablespoonfuls over top of apple mixture.

Sprinkle remaining 1 teaspoon granulated sugar over topping. Bake 35 minutes or until topping is lightly browned and apples are tender. Cool buckle slightly in pan on wire rack.

Combine apple butter and liqueur in small microwavable bowl. Microwave at HIGH 1 minute or until warm. Spoon 1 to 2 tablespoonfuls sauce over each serving. Garnish with mint leaves, if desired. *Makes 8 servings*

Apple Cranberry Buckle

STRAWBERRY RHUBARB PIE

Pastry for double-crust 9-inch pie
4 cups sliced (1-inch pieces) fresh rhubarb
3 cups (1 pint) fresh strawberries, sliced
1½ cups granulated sugar
½ cup cornstarch
2 tablespoons quick-cooking tapioca
1 tablespoon grated lemon peel
¼ teaspoon ground allspice
1 egg, lightly beaten

Preheat oven to 425°F. Roll out half the pastry; place in 9-inch pie plate. Trim pastry; flute edges, sealing to edge of pie plate. Set aside. Place fruit in large bowl. In medium bowl, combine sugar, cornstarch, tapioca, lemon peel and allspice; mix well. Sprinkle sugar mixture over fruit; toss to coat well. Fill pie shell evenly with fruit. (Do not mound in center.) Roll out remaining pastry to 10-inch circle. Cut into ½-inch-wide strips. Form into lattice design over fruit. Brush egg over pastry. Bake 50 minutes or until filling is bubbly and thick. Cool on wire rack. Serve warm or at room temperature.

Makes 8 servings

FRESH BERRY COBBLER CAKE

1 pint fresh berries (blueberries, blackberries, raspberries and/or strawberries)
1 cup all-purpose flour
1¼ cups sugar, divided
1 teaspoon baking powder
¼ teaspoon salt
3 tablespoons butter or margarine
½ cup milk
1 tablespoon cornstarch
1 cup cold water
Additional berries (optional)

Preheat oven to 375°F. Place 1 pint berries in 9×9-inch baking pan; set aside. Combine flour, ½ cup sugar, baking powder and salt in large bowl. Cut in butter with pastry blender or two knives until coarse crumbs form. Stir in milk. Spoon over berries. Combine remaining ¾ cup sugar and cornstarch in small bowl. Stir in water until sugar mixture dissolves; pour over berry mixture. Bake 35 to 40 minutes or until lightly browned. Serve warm or cool completely. Garnish with additional berries, if desired.

Makes 6 servings

Favorite recipe from **Bob Evans®**

Strawberry Rhubarb Pie

GINGERBREAD UPSIDE–DOWN CAKE

1 can (20 ounces) DOLE® Pineapple Slices
½ cup margarine, softened, divided
1 cup packed brown sugar, divided
10 maraschino cherries
1 egg
½ cup dark molasses
1½ cups all-purpose flour
1 teaspoon baking soda
1 teaspoon ground ginger
½ teaspoon ground cinnamon
½ teaspoon salt

• Preheat oven to 350°F. Drain pineapple; reserve ½ cup syrup. In 10-inch cast iron skillet, melt ¼ cup margarine. Remove from heat. Stir in ½ cup brown sugar. Top with pineapple slices. Place 1 cherry in center of each slice.

• In large mixer bowl, beat remaining ¼ cup margarine and ½ cup brown sugar until fluffy. Beat in egg and molasses. In bowl, combine dry ingredients.

• In saucepan, bring reserved pineapple syrup to a boil. Add dry ingredients to creamed mixture alternately with syrup. Spread over pineapple in skillet. Bake 30 to 40 minutes or until wooden pick inserted in center comes out clean. Cool on wire rack 5 minutes. Invert onto serving plate.

Makes 8 to 10 servings

CINNAMON–SPICE APPLE CRISP

1½ pounds tart baking apples
1 tablespoon lemon juice
2 tablespoons granulated sugar
⅔ cup packed light brown sugar
½ cup all-purpose flour
⅓ cup quick-cooking oats
½ teaspoon ground cinnamon
¼ teaspoon ground nutmeg
¼ teaspoon ground ginger
¼ teaspoon ground mace
5 tablespoons cold butter or margarine, cut into pieces

1. Preheat oven to 375°F.

2. Mix apples, lemon juice and granulated sugar in large bowl; arrange in ungreased 1½-quart glass casserole.

3. Combine brown sugar, flour, oats, cinnamon, nutmeg, ginger and mace in medium bowl. Cut in margarine with pastry blender or 2 knives until mixture resembles coarse crumbs. Sprinkle brown sugar mixture over apples.

4. Bake, uncovered, about 30 minutes or until apples are tender and topping is golden. Serve warm with frozen yogurt, if desired. Sprinkle with additional ground cinnamon, if desired.

Makes 6 servings

Cinnamon-Spice Apple Crisp

SOUR CREAM POUND CAKE

1 cup butter, softened
2¾ cups sugar
1 tablespoon vanilla
2 teaspoons grated orange peel
6 eggs
3 cups all-purpose flour
½ teaspoon salt
¼ teaspoon baking soda
1 cup sour cream
Citrus Topping (recipe follows)

Preheat oven to 325°F. Grease 10-inch tube pan. Beat butter in large bowl with electric mixer at medium speed until creamy. Gradually add sugar, beating until light and fluffy. Beat in vanilla and orange peel. Add eggs, 1 at a time, beating 1 minute after each addition. Combine flour, salt and baking soda in small bowl. Add to butter mixture alternately with sour cream, beginning and ending with flour mixture. Beat well after each addition. Pour into prepared pan. Bake 1 hour and 15 minutes or until cake tester or wooden skewer inserted in center comes out clean.

Meanwhile, prepare Citrus Topping. Spoon over hot cake; cool in pan 15 minutes. Remove from pan to wire rack; cool completely.

Makes 10 to 12 servings

CITRUS TOPPING

2 oranges
2 teaspoons salt
Water
½ cup sugar, divided
⅓ cup lemon juice
1 teaspoon vanilla

Zest peel of oranges to measure ⅓ cup. Combine orange peel and salt in medium saucepan. Add enough water to cover. Bring to a boil over high heat. Boil 2 minutes. Drain in fine-meshed sieve. Return orange peel to saucepan. Add orange juice and ¼ cup sugar to saucepan. Bring to a boil over high heat. Reduce heat; simmer 10 minutes. Remove from heat. Add remaining ¼ cup sugar, lemon juice and vanilla; stir until smooth.

TIP

Before grating or zesting lemon peel, wash lemons with warm, soapy water to remove wax and any traces of insecticide.

Sour Cream Pound Cake

CARROT CAKE

CAKE
1¼ **pounds carrots, scraped and cut lengthwise into 2-inch pieces (about 8 to 10 medium carrots)***
2 **cups granulated sugar**
1½ **CRISCO® Sticks or 1½ cups CRISCO® all-vegetable shortening plus additional for greasing**
4 **eggs**
½ **cup water**
2 **cups all-purpose flour**
1 **tablespoon ground cinnamon**
2 **teaspoons baking soda**
1 **teaspoon salt**

FROSTING
1 **package (8 ounces) cream cheese, softened**
½ **Butter Flavor** CRISCO® Stick or ½ cup Butter Flavor** CRISCO® all-vegetable shortening**
1 **box (1 pound) confectioners' sugar (3½ to 4 cups)**
1 **teaspoon pure vanilla extract**
¼ **teaspoon salt**

GARNISH (OPTIONAL)
Chopped nuts
Carrot curls

Grate carrots very finely if food processor is unavailable.

**Butter Flavor Crisco® is artificially flavored.*

1. Heat oven to 350°F. Grease 13×9×2-inch insulated pan with shortening. Flour lightly.

2. For cake, place carrots in food processor. Process until very fine. Measure 3 cups carrots.

3. Combine granulated sugar and 1½ cups shortening in large bowl. Beat at medium speed of electric mixer until creamy. Beat in eggs until blended. Beat in water at low speed until blended.

4. Combine flour, cinnamon, baking soda and 1 teaspoon salt in medium bowl. Add to creamed mixture. Beat at low speed until blended. Beat 2 minutes at medium speed. Add carrots. Beat until well blended. Pour into pan.

5. Bake at 350°F for 40 to 55 minutes or until toothpick inserted in center comes out clean. *Do not overbake.* Cool 10 minutes. Invert onto wire rack. Cool completely.

6. For frosting, combine cream cheese and ½ cup shortening in large bowl. Beat at medium speed until blended. Reduce speed to low. Add confectioners' sugar, vanilla and ¼ teaspoon salt. Beat until blended. Beat at medium speed until frosting is of desired spreading consistency. Frost cake.

Makes 12 to 16 servings

If cake is baked in non-insulated pan, baking time will be shorter. Test for doneness at minimum baking time.

Carrot Cake

CHOCOLATE MAYONNAISE CAKE

2 cups all-purpose flour
²⁄₃ cup unsweetened cocoa
1¼ teaspoons baking soda
¼ teaspoon baking powder
3 eggs
1²⁄₃ cups sugar
1 teaspoon vanilla
1 cup HELLMANN'S® or BEST FOODS® Real or Light Mayonnaise
1¹⁄₃ cups water

1. Preheat oven to 350°F. Grease and flour bottoms of two 9×1½-inch round cake pans.

2. In medium bowl, combine flour, cocoa, baking soda and baking powder; set aside.

3. In large bowl with mixer at high speed, beat eggs, sugar and vanilla, scraping bowl occasionally, 3 minutes or until smooth and creamy. Reduce speed to low; beat in mayonnaise until blended. Add flour mixture in 4 additions alternately with water, beginning and ending with flour mixture. Pour into prepared pans.

4. Bake 30 to 35 minutes or until cake springs back when touched lightly in center. Cool in pans on wire racks 10 minutes. Remove from pans; cool completely on racks. Fill and frost as desired.

Makes 1 (9-inch) layer cake

RICE PUDDING

3 cups 2% low-fat milk
1 large stick cinnamon
1 cup uncooked rice*
2 cups water
½ teaspoon salt
    Peel of orange or lemon
¾ cup sugar
¼ cup raisins
2 tablespoons dark rum

*Recipe based on regular-milled long grain white rice.

Heat milk and cinnamon in small saucepan over medium heat until milk is infused with flavor of cinnamon, about 15 minutes. Combine rice, water, and salt in 2- to 3-quart saucepan. Bring to a boil; stir once or twice. Place orange peel on top of rice. Reduce heat; cover and simmer 15 minutes or until rice is tender and liquid is absorbed. Remove and discard orange peel. Strain milk and stir into cooked rice. Add sugar and simmer 20 minutes or until thickened, stirring often. Add raisins and rum; simmer 10 minutes. Serve hot. To reheat, add a little milk to restore creamy texture.   *Makes 6 servings*

Tip: Use medium or short grain rice for rice pudding for a creamier consistency.

Favorite recipe from **USA Rice Federation**

Rice Pudding

GERMAN HONEY BARS (LEBKUCHEN)

2¾ cups all-purpose flour
  2 teaspoons ground cinnamon
  1 teaspoon baking powder
  ½ teaspoon baking soda
  ½ teaspoon salt
  ½ teaspoon ground cardamom
  ½ teaspoon ground ginger
  ½ cup honey
  ½ cup dark molasses
  ¾ cup packed brown sugar
  3 tablespoons butter, melted
  1 large egg
  ½ cup chopped toasted
      almonds (optional)
      Glaze (recipe follows)

Preheat oven to 350°F. Grease 15×10-inch jelly-roll pan; set aside. Combine flour, cinnamon, baking powder, baking soda, salt, cardamom and ginger in medium bowl. Combine honey and molasses in medium saucepan; bring to a boil over medium heat. Remove from heat; cool 10 minutes. Stir in brown sugar, butter and egg.

Place brown sugar mixture in large bowl. Gradually add flour mixture. Beat at low speed with electric mixer until dough forms. Stir in almonds with spoon, if desired. (Dough will be slightly sticky.) Spread dough evenly into prepared pan. Bake 20 to 22 minutes or until golden brown and set. Remove pan to wire rack; cool completely.

Prepare Glaze. Spread over cooled bar cookies. Let stand until set, about 30 minutes. Cut into 2×1-inch bars. Store tightly covered at room temperature or freeze up to 3 months.

Makes about 6 dozen bars

GLAZE

1¼ cups powdered sugar
  3 tablespoons fresh lemon
      juice
  1 teaspoon grated lemon peel

Place all ingredients in medium bowl; stir with spoon until smooth.

 TIP

To toast nuts, spread them in single layer on a baking sheet and toast them in a preheated 350°F oven for 8 to 10 minutes. Watch carefully and stir them once or twice for even browning.

German Honey Bars (Lebkuchen)

PINEAPPLE RAISIN JUMBLES

2 cans (8 ounces each) DOLE®
   Crushed Pineapple
½ cup margarine, softened
½ cup sugar
1 teaspoon vanilla extract
1 cup all-purpose flour
4 teaspoons grated orange
   peel
1 cup DOLE® Blanched
   Slivered Almonds, toasted
1 cup DOLE® Seedless Raisins

• Preheat oven to 350°F. Drain pineapple well, pressing out excess liquid with back of spoon.

• In large bowl, beat margarine and sugar until light and fluffy. Stir in pineapple and vanilla. Beat in flour and orange peel. Stir in almonds and raisins.

• Drop heaping tablespoons of dough 2 inches apart onto greased cookie sheets.

• Bake 20 to 22 minutes or until firm. Cool on wire racks.
   Makes 2 to 2½ dozen cookies

CHOCOLATE DROP SUGAR COOKIES

⅔ cup butter or margarine,
   softened
1 cup sugar
1 egg
1½ teaspoons vanilla extract
1½ cups all-purpose flour
½ cup HERSHEY'S Cocoa
½ teaspoon baking soda
¼ teaspoon salt
⅓ cup buttermilk or sour milk*
   Additional sugar

To sour milk: Use 1 teaspoon white vinegar plus milk to equal ⅓ cup.

1. Heat oven to 350°F. Lightly grease cookie sheet.

2. Beat butter and sugar in large bowl until well blended. Add egg and vanilla; beat until light and fluffy. Stir together flour, cocoa, baking soda and salt; add alternately with buttermilk to butter mixture. Using ice cream scoop or ¼ cup measuring cup, drop dough about 2 inches apart onto prepared cookie sheet.

3. Bake 13 to 15 minutes or until cookie springs back when touched lightly in center. While cookies are on cookie sheet, sprinkle lightly with additional sugar. Cool slightly; remove from cookie sheet to wire rack. Cool completely.
   Makes about 1 dozen cookies

COCOA SNICKERDOODLES

1 cup butter, softened
¾ cup packed brown sugar
¾ cup plus 2 tablespoons
    granulated sugar, divided
2 eggs
2 cups uncooked rolled oats
1½ cups all-purpose flour
¼ cup plus 2 tablespoons
    unsweetened cocoa
    powder, divided
1 teaspoon baking soda
2 tablespoons ground
    cinnamon

Preheat oven to 375°F. Lightly grease cookie sheets or line with parchment paper.

Beat butter, brown sugar and ¾ cup granulated sugar in large bowl until light and fluffy. Add eggs; mix well. Combine oats, flour, ¼ cup cocoa and baking soda in medium bowl. Stir into butter mixture until blended.

Mix remaining 2 tablespoons granulated sugar, remaining 2 tablespoons cocoa and cinnamon in small bowl. Drop dough by rounded teaspoonfuls into cinnamon mixture; toss to coat. Place 2 inches apart on prepared cookie sheets.

Bake 8 to 10 minutes or until firm in center. *Do not overbake.* Remove to wire racks to cool.
    Makes about 4½ dozen cookies

PFEFFERNUSSE

3½ cups all-purpose flour
2 teaspoons baking powder
1½ teaspoons ground cinnamon
1 teaspoon ground ginger
½ teaspoon baking soda
½ teaspoon salt
½ teaspoon ground cloves
½ teaspoon ground cardamom
¼ teaspoon freshly ground
    black pepper
1 cup butter, softened
1 cup granulated sugar
¼ cup dark molasses
1 egg
    Powdered sugar

Combine flour, baking powder, cinnamon, ginger, baking soda, salt, cloves, cardamom and pepper in large bowl.

Beat butter and sugar in large bowl with electric mixer at medium speed until light and fluffy. Beat in molasses and egg. Gradually add flour mixture. Beat at low speed until dough forms. Shape dough into disk; wrap in plastic wrap and refrigerate until firm, 30 minutes or up to 3 days.

Preheat oven to 350°F. Grease cookie sheets. Roll dough into 1-inch balls. Place 2 inches apart on prepared cookie sheets.

Bake 12 to 14 minutes or until golden brown. Transfer cookies to wire racks; dust with sifted powdered sugar. Cool completely.
    Makes about 60 cookies

OATMEAL TREASURES

COOKIES

3/4 **Butter Flavor* CRISCO®
Stick or 3/4 cup Butter
Flavor CRISCO® all-
vegtable shortening plus
additional for greasing**
1 1/4 **cups firmly packed light
brown sugar**
1 **egg**
1/3 **cup milk**
1 1/2 **teaspoons vanilla**
3 **cups quick oats, uncooked**
1 **cup all-purpose flour**
1/2 **teaspoon baking soda**
1/2 **teaspoon salt**
1 **cup milk chocolate chips**
1/2 **cup flake coconut**

DRIZZLE

1/3 **cup white chocolate baking
pieces**
1 **tablespoon plus 2 teaspoons
Butter Flavor* CRISCO®
Stick or 1 tablespoon plus
2 teaspoons Butter
Flavor* CRISCO®, divided**
1/3 **cup semi-sweet chocolate
chips**

**Butter Flavor Crisco® is artifically
flavored.*

1. Heat oven to 375°F. Grease
baking sheets with shortening.
Place sheets of foil on countertop
for cooling cookies.

2. For cookies, combine 3/4 cup
shortening, brown sugar, egg, milk
and vanilla in large bowl. Beat at
medium speed of electric mixer
until well blended.

3. Combine oats, flour, baking
soda and salt. Mix into creamed
mixture at low speed just until
blended. Stir in chips and
coconut.

4. Drop rounded tablespoonfuls of
dough 2 inches apart onto
ungreased baking sheet.

5. Bake one baking sheet at a time
at 375°F for 10 to 12 minutes or
until lightly browned. *Do not
overbake.* Cool 2 minutes on
baking sheet. Remove cookies to
foil to cool completely.

6. For drizzle, place white
chocolate pieces and 1
tablespoon shortening in heavy
resealable plastic bag or
microwave-safe bowl. Microwave
at 50% (MEDIUM) for 1 minute.
Knead or stir and repeat, if
necessary, until completely
smooth. Cut tiny tip off corner of
bag. Drizzle over top of each
cookie. Melt semi-sweet chocolate
chips and remaining 2 teaspoon
shortening as directed for white
chocolate. Drizzle again over top
of each cookie.
   Makes about 2 1/2 dozen cookies

ACKNOWLEDGMENTS

The publishers would like to thank the companies and organizations listed below for the use of their recipes in this publication.

Bestfoods

Birds Eye®

Bob Evans®

Campbell Soup Company

Dole Food Company, Inc.

Golden Grain®

Grey Poupon® Mustard

Heinz U.S.A.

Hershey Foods Corporation

Hunt-Wesson, Inc.

Land O' Lakes, Inc.

Lawry's® Foods, Inc.

Lipton®

National Honey Board

Perdue Farms Incorporated

The Procter & Gamble Company

Reckitt & Colman Inc.

The J.M. Smucker Company

Uncle Ben's Inc.

USA Rice Federation

INDEX

INDEX

METRIC CONVERSION CHART

VOLUME MEASUREMENTS (dry)

⅛ teaspoon = 0.5 mL
¼ teaspoon = 1 mL
½ teaspoon = 2 mL
¾ teaspoon = 4 mL
1 teaspoon = 5 mL
1 tablespoon = 15 mL
2 tablespoons = 30 mL
¼ cup = 60 mL
⅓ cup = 75 mL
½ cup = 125 mL
⅔ cup = 150 mL
¾ cup = 175 mL
1 cup = 250 mL
2 cups = 1 pint = 500 mL
3 cups = 750 mL
4 cups = 1 quart = 1 L

VOLUME MEASUREMENTS (fluid)

1 fluid ounce (2 tablespoons) = 30 mL
4 fluid ounces (½ cup) = 125 mL
8 fluid ounces (1 cup) = 250 mL
12 fluid ounces (1½ cups) = 375 mL
16 fluid ounces (2 cups) = 500 mL

WEIGHTS (mass)

½ ounce = 15 g
1 ounce = 30 g
3 ounces = 90 g
4 ounces = 120 g
8 ounces = 225 g
10 ounces = 285 g
12 ounces = 360 g
16 ounces = 1 pound = 450 g

DIMENSIONS

1/16 inch = 2 mm
⅛ inch = 3 mm
¼ inch = 6 mm
½ inch = 1.5 cm
¾ inch = 2 cm
1 inch = 2.5 cm

OVEN TEMPERATURES

250°F = 120°C
275°F = 140°C
300°F = 150°C
325°F = 160°C
350°F = 180°C
375°F = 190°C
400°F = 200°C
425°F = 220°C
450°F = 230°C

BAKING PAN SIZES

Utensil	Size in Inches/Quarts	Metric Volume	Size in Centimeters
Baking or Cake Pan (square or rectangular)	8×8×2	2 L	20×20×5
	9×9×2	2.5 L	23×23×5
	12×8×2	3 L	30×20×5
	13×9×2	3.5 L	33×23×5
Loaf Pan	8×4×3	1.5 L	20×10×7
	9×5×3	2 L	23×13×7
Round Layer Cake Pan	8×1½	1.2 L	20×4
	9×1½	1.5 L	23×4
Pie Plate	8×1¼	750 mL	20×3
	9×1¼	1 L	23×3
Baking Dish or Casserole	1 quart	1 L	—
	1½ quart	1.5 L	—
	2 quart	2 L	—